SISTERS
a photographic celebration

BOK4061

A sister is a little bit of

childhood that can

never be lost.

Marion C. Garretty

Your sister will be the first to criticize you

but if anyone else tries to, your sister will

defend you until the end of the world.

Lisette Favier

Even when you are sixty, you

are still six to your sister.

Pam Brown

To be sisters and friends

is happiness doubled.

Anonymous

There can be no situation in life in which

the conversation of my dear sister will

not administer some comfort to me.

Lady Mary Wortley Montagu

"Sisters" is probably the most

competitive relationship within

the family, but once the sisters

are grown, it becomes the

strongest relationship.

Margaret Mead

The growth of true friendship

may be a lifelong affair.

Sarah Orne Jewett

For there is no friend like a sister

In calm or stormy weather;

To cheer one on the tedious way,

To fetch one if one goes astray,

To lift one if one totters down,

To strengthen whilst one stands.

Christina Rossetti

A sister is always there to

defend you no matter what.

Felicity Martin

There's a special kind of freedom sisters enjoy.

Anonymous

Having a sister means having one

of the most beautiful and unique

of human relationships.

Anonymous

Friendship is a sheltering tree.

Samuel Taylor Coleridge

Where there's a sibling there's quibbling.

Selma Raskin

A sister is one of the nicest things

that can happen to anyone.

Anonymous

All who joy would win

Must share it—happiness was born a twin.

Lord Byron

Sisters don't come and go; sisters are with you inside and out, from the time you were weaned to the time you die. Boyfriends have nothing on sisters.

Franny Hammont

We are each other's

reference point at

our turning points.

Elizabeth Fishel

There is space within sisterhood for likeness

and difference, for the subtle differences

that challenge and delight; there is space

for disappointment—and surprise.

Christine Downing

Lord help the mister that comes

between me and my sister...

Irving Berlin

A sister is both your mirror

and your opposite.

Elizabeth Fishel

She is your witness,

who sees you at your worst

and best,

and loves you anyway.

Barbara Alpert

Remember, we all stumble,

every one of us. That's why it's

a comfort to go hand-in-hand.

Anonymous

Go ahead, dive in.

Sisterhood gives one courage.

Lulu Colebrook

Sisters by chance.

Friends by choice.

Anonymous

It was from you that I first learned

to think,

to feel,

to imagine,

to believe…

John Sterling

Never let an angry sister

comb your hair.

Patricia McCann

They fall in and out ten times a day,

just as though they were man and wife.

Oliver Goldsmith

...a sister is naggings and needlings,

whispers and whispering. Bribery.

Thumpings. Borrowings. Breakings.

Kisses and cuddling. Lending.

Surprises. Defendings and comfortings.

Welcomings home.

Pam Brown

In thee my soul shall own combined

The sistcr and the friend.

Catherine Killigrow

Sisters are known for sharing

laughter and wiping tears.

Anonymous

You can tell your sister secrets, you tell your

sister you've scraped the car, you even tell

your sister that you hate your sister (course,

that bit's not true)—mainly, because you

can tell your sister everything.

Jas Nathan

One's sister is a part of one's essential self,

an eternal presence of one's heart,

soul and memory.

Susan Cahil

Never underestimate the harmony of sisterhood

Lulu Colebrook

There's something beautiful about finding

one's innermost thoughts in another.

Olive Schreiner

Only a sister can compare the sleek

body that now exists with the

chubby body hidden underneath.

Only a sister knows about former

pimples, failing math, and

underwear kicked under the bed.

Laura Tracy

A joy shared is a joy doubled.

Johann Wolfgang von Goethe

Love and joy are twins,

or born of each other.

William Hazlitt

Having a sister means that

you'll never be left alone in

life, or left alone by your sister.

Felicity Martin

The best thing about

having a sister was that

I always had a friend.

Cali Rae Turner

I never asked for sisters,

they were just there.

Frances Grant

...my sisters have shown me

how to live.

Georgette Wasserstein

My sister taught me everything I need to know.

Linda Sunshine

We may look old and wise to the outside.

But to each other we are still in junior school.

Charlotte Gray

Big sisters are the creamer in your coffee.

Patricia McCann

[Having a sister is] like

having a best friend

around for your whole life.

Amanda Hector

No one knows better than

my sister how we grew up.

Dale V. Atkins

If your sister is in a tearing hurry to go

out and cannot catch your eye, she's

wearing your best sweater.

Pam Brown

No matter the problem

No matter the pain.

No matter the years that pass

Sisters will always be there.

Stuart and Linda Macfarlane

If ever I seem to take you

for granted, forgive me.

Helen Fitzwalter Read

Sisters don't come and go;

Sisters are with you inside and out.

Franny Hammont

103

The desire to be and have a sister is a
primitive and profound one...It is a desire
to know and be known by someone who
shares blood and body, history and dreams,
common ground and the unknown
adventures of the future, darkest secrets,
and the glassiest beads of truth.

Elizabeth Fishel

There's no fooling a sister—she can

always see right through any disguise.

Janet Goddard

A sister is dear to you
always, for she is someone
who is always a part of all
the favorite memories that
you keep close to your
heart.

Anonymous

Picture Credits

All images Hulton Getty Picture Collection.

cover: Sisters Dorothy, Iris, and Myra Tagg put their heads together for a spot of relaxation, 1937.

title page: Nona Georgette and Mary Litita, daughters of Lady Lawrence, circa 1925.

page 5: Wearing ruched swimsuits, three young sisters trail seaweed as they run through the shallows on the beach, 1956.

page 6: Popular vocal harmony group The Andrews Sisters, Maxene, Patty, and Laverne, 1945.

page 8: Two daughters of the Earl and Countess of Kinnoul on board their parents' steam trawler, 1936.

page 11: Portrait of American actors and sisters, Loretta, Polly Ann, and Elizabeth Jane Young, circa 1930.

page 13: Three elderly sisters light the birthday cake candles during a celebration to mark the 80th anniversary of Croyden High School for girls, 1954.

page 15: Actress sisters Betsy, Vicky, and Dixie Ross, 1946.

page 16: Baby Jeanne Whitham being nursed by sisters Ellen (11) and Molly (13), 1945.

page 18: Twin girls and their sister smile hopefully as they ask for this year's presents from Father Christmas, 1948.

page 20: A young boxer gives his sisters some hints on how to use the gloves, 1938.

page 22: Olamae and Lura Asah, two sisters wearing traditional tribal dress. The Asah sisters are native American indians, 1952.

page 24: A young girl cleaning her baby sister in the bath, 1948.

page 27: The athletic Grove sisters, from left to right: Dorothy, Brenda, Muriel, and Kathleen, 1933.

page 28: As a Christmas holiday art activity, Jennifer and Pamela Greenwood, draw exhibits at the Natural History Museum, 1961.

page 30: Sisters Dorothy, Iris, and Myra Tagg put their heads together for a spot of relaxation, 1937.

page 33: Pat and June Mackell, twin sisters aged 18, 1956.

page 34: Norwegian world champion ski jumper Johanne Kolstad and her sister Kitty at Earls Court, London, before the indoor skiing show "Cavalcade," 1938.

page 37: Queen Elizabeth II and her younger sister Princess Margaret sitting on the grass in the grounds of the Royal Lodge, Windsor, 1936.

page 38: Linda Murphy, aged 6, and her sister Jill, aged 4, in their nurses' uniforms that won them a special prize for sisters at a Fancy Dress Party, 1959.

page 40: 1st year psychology student Marie Goodman gets down on the floor to do some studying with a glass of milk and a few good books. She is the sister of fashion model Judy Goodman, 1962.

page 43: Nona Georgette and Mary Litita, daughters of Lady Lawrence, circa 1925.

page 44: Picture Post Personality Girl for June, Jocelyn Wardrop-Moore, fitting a dress on her sister, 1954.

page 46: Celine Flanagan helps her younger sister Karen learn how to skate, circa 1950.

page 49: Sisters Shirley (aged 4), Heather (aged 5), and Helen May (aged 6) poised to dive into the pool, 1937.

page 51: Golfing sisters Pat and Mary Ryder practicing their swings on the course at the Orsett Gold Club, 1954.

page 52: A teenager helping her younger sister with her

homework, circa 1955.

page 55: A little girl combs her sister's hair in preparation for a party to celebrate the coronation of Queen Elizabeth II, 1953.

page 56: A young boy cries as his sister mischievously showers him from a watering can, 1933.

page 59: Two sisters, Irene and Clive Hawthorne, who are to captain rival soccer teams, 1934.

page 60: Brenda Tarrant and her sister Barbara huddle together under a waterproof coat on the seafront on a windy day, 1962.

page 63: Two young sisters laughing, circa 1950.

page 64: Jocelyn Wardrop-Moore, Picture Post's "Personality Girl" of 1954, gives her sister a lift on her scooter, 1954.

page 67: Two young sisters, Maria and Conchita Gondar, feeding ducks in the park, circa 1955.

page 68: The vocal harmony group The Beverley Sisters: Joy (center) and her twin sisters Teddy and Babs, 1951.

page 71: Two young sisters take turns to weigh themselves on the bathroom scales, circa 1955.

page 72: Two sisters, Rita and Rosemary Algane, enjoying a game in the sun, 1953.

page 75: Two sisters playing, 1920.

page 76: Twins Leila and Valerie Croft at a ten pin bowling alley, 1960.

page 79: Two sisters watching the Thanksgiving Day Parade in New York, 1961.

page 80: Twin sisters and pianists Geraldine and Mary Peppin, 1943.

page 82: Three of the twenty children of record-breaking mother Elizabeth Hudson, sharing a bed, 1953.

page 84: The Fayre Sisters, a family of dancers and musicians, 1933.

page 87: Japanese sisters dressed in holiday clothes, circa 1930.

page 89: Elsie and Doris Waters, the two sisters who perfected a comedy act as "Gert" and "Daisy," circa 1954.

page 90: Seven-year-old Susan Good helps one of her quadruplet sisters dry her hands as she gets ready for school, 1953.

page 92: The Debenham sisters wearing fur coats and riding motorbikes, 1925.

page 95: Inuit sisters from Unalakleet, aged seven and ten, circa 1955.

page 96: The Morley sisters Molly and Kitty, 1932.

page 98: Twin sisters Nancy and Kitty Yates with two pupils who are also twins, 1934.

page 101: Mrs Gladys Burne and Mrs Beryl Richardson, 1976.

page 102: The five-year-old Good quadruplets—Jennifer, Bridget, Elizabeth, and Frances—with their big sister, Susan, age 7, 1953.

page 105: The three sisters of his highness King Zog of Albania, 1938.

page 107: Two sisters as "The Artist and 'his' Portrait," 1954.

page 109: The three young Mawby triplets, Claudette, Angela, and Claudine, say their prayers before bed, 1932.

Copyright © 2002 MQ Publications Limited

This edition published in 2002 by MQ Publications exclusively for Hallmark Cards, Inc.

www.hallmark.com

Library of Congress Cataloguing-in-Publication Data

CIP data has been applied for.

Printed and bound in China

5 6 7 8 9 10

Cover design: John Casey
Design: Alexia Smith
Text and picture research: Suzie Green
Series Editor: Elizabeth Carr